PRINCETON LEGENDS ALPHABET

Words by Robin Feiner

A is for **A**lan Turing. Cracking Germany's 'unbreakable' Enigma code, this brilliant Princeton math major helped end World War II. Thanks to his pioneering work developing the first modern computer, he transformed how we live and work today. He also set the benchmark for AI with his famous Turing Test.

B is for Jeff **B**ezos. Launched in 1994 from a garage, Amazon has grown into a global giant, revolutionized how we shop, and made Bezos one of the world's richest people. Jeff donates much of his wealth to fight climate change and homelessness. No wonder he's considered Princeton's most influential graduate.

is for Charles 'Pete' Conrad. Daring to go where few men have—space— Conrad became the first Ivy League astronaut. Commanding the Apollo 12 space mission in 1969, he walked on the moon, and continued his stellar career as the first American commander of a manned space station. For Princeton graduates, not even the sky's the limit.

D is for **D**avid Remnick. A fearless writer and journalist, Remnick took the helm of The New Yorker in 1998, making him one of the most admired people in the publishing world. Modernizing the magazine, he shaped it into a publication exemplifying Princeton's commitment to free thinking and accuracy.

E is for **E**than Coen. Graduating with a philosophy diploma, Ethan—one half of the Coen brothers—joined New York's creative scene. Soon, the Coen brothers' first film hit the big screen, forcing Hollywood to take notice. Now, Ethan has six Academy Awards and a Palme d'Or to his name.

F is for Steve **F**orbes.
At Princeton, Steve did
what members of the Forbes
family do—he founded
Business Today, which is
currently the largest student-
run magazine in the world.
Steve eventually became
editor-in-chief of the Forbes
business magazine before
running two campaigns
for president!

G is for **G**ita Gopinath. Blazing a path from Kolkata to the USA, Gita stopped at Princeton to earn her Ph.D. in Economics. She's the first Indian woman to be appointed as a full professor in Harvard's School of Economics and the first female chief economist of the International Monetary Fund.

H is for Mellody Hobson. 'Don't be afraid to be yourself. Be that person. Speak your truth,' advises this influential Princeton graduate. Wise words from an inspiring woman who has risen through the ranks to president and co-CEO of Ariel Investments while simultaneously serving as the chairwoman of Starbucks.

I is for Lee **I**acocca.
As the father of the Ford Mustang, Lee made himself a household name. Working his magic at the Chrysler Corporation, he rescued the company from bankruptcy. Later, Iacocca raised millions of dollars to restore Lady Liberty for her 100th anniversary.

Jj

**J is for Jimmy Stewart.
Launching his legendary
film and stage career soon
after graduating, Stewart
earned recognition with
lifetime achievement awards
at both the Oscars and
Golden Globes. Jimmy
maintained close connections
to Princeton, and the
university honored him
with its James Stewart
Film Theater.**

Kk

K is for Wendy Kopp. Embracing Princeton's motto of service to humanity, this visionary created a plan to address educational inequity. Teach for All recruits top-tier college grads and uses their talents in the classroom, ensuring students across the globe have the opportunities they deserve.

L is for Jim **L**ee.
As a psychology graduate, this Princetonian landed a job at Marvel Comics. It wasn't long before he had penciled and co-written X-Men #1— the best-selling comic book of all time. In 2018, Lee was promoted to Chief Creative Officer of DC Comics and is now as famous as the superheroes he draws.

M is for **M**eg Whitman. The first woman ever to serve as CEO of two Fortune 500 companies, Whitman oversaw eBay's growth from a startup to multibillion-dollar business, and at HP she turned their fortunes around. Meg credits Princeton's influence for guiding her throughout her working life.

N is for **N**orman Thomas. This valedictorian from the Class of 1905 went on to become a six-time presidential candidate. He fearlessly spoke out in favor of civil rights and liberties, earning the nickname 'America's Conscience.' For his bold attacks on segregation, Martin Luther King, Jr. called him 'the bravest man I ever met.'

O is for Michelle **O**bama. First Lady, Mom-in-Chief, lawyer, author. During her White House years, she inspired others with her Let's Move! public health campaign and her focus on education. Michelle extends her message to everyone: be your best self. Legendary!

P is for Jodi **P**icoult.
At Princeton, Picoult learned to craft her gift for story-telling into page-turners. With 28 titles published in 34 languages, Jodi's books have now sold over 40 million copies worldwide. She's become a book club icon who fearlessly raises social awareness about challenging issues.

Q is for Queen Noor of Jordan. Embodying Princeton's motto, 'in service of humanity,' Noor Al-Hussein devotes herself to many worthy causes, including presiding over the United World Colleges. She's even been decorated with Princeton's own Woodrow Wilson Award for her public service.

R is for Maria **R**essa. After earning her degree in English with certificates in theater and dance, this bold journalist returned home to the Philippines to fight for freedom of expression. Winning the Nobel Peace Prize for her efforts, Maria credits her Princeton education for her accomplishments.

S is for **S**onia Sotomayor. Entering Princeton's famed FitzRandolph Gateway, Sotomayor began fulfilling her dream. 33 years later, President Obama nominated her for the Supreme Court, where she has served as the nation's first Hispanic justice. 'Be different, be brave, be you!' writes Sonia in one of her many published works.

T is for **T**erence Tao. Attending Princeton on a Fulbright Scholarship, this child prodigy was awarded his Ph.D. at just 21 years of age. Often referred to as the 'Mozart of Math,' Terence is considered one of the world's greatest living mathematicians, and even has a Fields Medal to his credit.

U is for Francis Robbins **U**pton. After earning Princeton's first Master of Science degree, this alum was recruited by none other than Thomas Edison. He provided the calculations necessary for developing the incandescent light bulb, and went on to patent the first electric fire alarm and fire detector.

V is for Robert Charles
Venturi Jr. Two degrees
from Princeton, along with
creativity and innovation,
have established Venturi as
a major architectural talent
of the 20th century. Having
designed four structures for
the university, he left a legacy
of 'warmth, wit, and courage'
for all to enjoy on the
Princeton campus.

W is for **W**oodrow Wilson. As the 28th president of the USA, Wilson was awarded the Nobel Peace Prize. Returning to his alma mater as the 13th President of Princeton University, he left an indelible mark by establishing the university's preceptorial system, a Princeton tradition that students still use today.

X is for Jenny **Xie.** Studying under Princeton's world-class writers, Xie explored her love of literature and honed her craft as a poet. Since, she has been a finalist for the National Book Award and has received the Walt Whitman Award from the Academy of American Poets.

Y is for E. Lily Yu.
**This rising literary star
is breaking barriers and
stretching the limits of
literature. Not one to give
up, Yu spent years revising
her first novel, rewriting it
three times. Once published,
the book was proclaimed
'devastating and perfect'
by The New York Times.**

Zz

Z is for Donna **Z**uckerberg. Her love for the classics motivated this determined 2014 Princeton Ph.D. graduate to create an award-winning publication exploring new ways of thinking about classical literature and feminism. Zuckerberg's first book won her praise as a fearless and outspoken pioneer.